Wicca For Beginners

The Guide to Wiccan Beliefs, Magic, Rituals, Witchcraft, and Living a Magical Life

PUBLISHED BY: Amy White
© Copyright 2019 - All rights reserved.

The content contained within this book may not be reproduced, duplicated or transmitted without direct written permission from the author or the publisher.

Under no circumstances will any blame or legal responsibility be held against the publisher, or author, for any damages, reparation, or monetary loss due to the information contained within this book. Either directly or indirectly.

Legal Notice:

This book is copyright protected. This book is only for personal use. You cannot amend, distribute, sell, use, quote or paraphrase any part, or the content within this book, without the consent of the author or publisher.

Disclaimer Notice:

Please note the information contained within this document is for educational and entertainment purposes only. All effort has been executed to present accurate, up to date, and reliable, complete information. No warranties of any kind are declared or implied. Readers acknowledge that the author is not engaging in the rendering of legal, financial, medical or professional advice. The content within this book has been derived from various sources. Please consult a licensed professional before attempting any techniques outlined in this book.

By reading this document, the reader agrees that under no circumstances is the author responsible for any losses, direct or indirect, which are incurred as a result of the use of information contained within this document, including, but not limited to, — errors, omissions, or inaccuracies

Table of Contents

My FREE Gifts to You 4
Introduction 5

PART 1: Introduction to Wicca **9**
Chapter 1: What is Wicca? 10
Chapter 2: Wiccan Beliefs 21
Chapter 3: Other Beliefs 41

PART 2: Introduction to Witchcraft **50**
Chapter 4: What is Witchcraft? 51
Chapter 5: Ritual and Spellwork 61

PART 3: Practical Wicca **77**
Chapter 6: Becoming a Wiccan 78
Chapter 7: Spells 86
Closure 98

Thank you! 102

My FREE Gifts to You

As a way of saying thanks for reading my book, I want to offer you my complete *Law of Attraction: Attract What You Desire* Boxset for FREE.

To get instant access just go to:

https://theartofmastery.com/loa

This boxset includes:

1. *Law of Attraction: Attract What You Desire* eBook
2. *Law of Attraction: Attract What You Desire* audiobook
3. LOA workbook with guided exercises
4. LOA checklist
5. Mind maps
6. 20 of the best LOA quotes posters
7. 20 of the best LOA affirmation posters

Get instant access at

https://theartofmastery.com/loa

Introduction

At a time when more and more doctors give out "nature prescriptions" because being close to green spaces makes you less depressed, boosts your immunity, and inspires your creativity, is it surprising that nature-venerating movements are gaining in popularity?

As people become more conscious of the consequences of living an unbalanced life, they seek a way of life, including a way of worshipping, that will help them find harmony both within themselves and with their environment.

There are many ways to practice Wicca and many different traditions to choose from, however, one thing they all have in common is reverence of Nature. If you can spiritually connect with animals, plants, natural elements, or landscapes, it will be easy to draw energy and guidance from them.

So, how do you promote balanced living and become a part of the web of life? You can start by harmonizing yourself with the natural cycles, and one of the ways of achieving that is by following the Wiccan calendar and observing the Sabbats.

The eight seasonal festivals mark the time of the year when major changes take place in Nature. For this reason, Wiccans consider Sabbats as auspicious times to tap into the energy of Mother Earth and bring changes into your own life.

The highlight of the Wiccan year, and the most important of all the Sabbats, is the Samhain, the Festival of the Dead. This Sabbat also marks the beginning of the Wiccan New Year and many Wiccans use it to perform rituals which help them turn a new leaf in their lives.

Rituals are essential to Wicca, and while you can do them successfully in the privacy of your home, whenever possible, Wiccans worship outdoors. The trick with Wicca rituals is to match your intent with both the Moon phases and the Elements, as well as with colors and symbols that represent each of the Elements.

For example, during the New or Waxing Moon, you can cast spells to boost new projects or relationships, while during the Waning Moon it's best to do spells to get rid of something or someone, such as debt or an unpleasant person.

Then, if you do a spell concerning money matters, you will want to focus on the Element of Earth and use symbols and colors that represent this element, such as crystals, leaves, or cones in brown or dark yellow color. While performing the ritual, you should be facing North.

Two major goals of all Wiccans are to live in harmony with Nature and to develop their intuition. Unlike most religions, which have strict rules on how things should be done and how festivals should be marked, Wicca encourages their members to develop and nurture their intuition and use it to find the best way to commune with the world of spirit. Therefore, instructions you find in this book concerning certain rituals are only a guideline and you should use your intuition to connect with a deity, an Element, or a season.

And finally, regardless of what many people think, Wiccans practice White magic and their spells are not meant to cause harm. Most of the spells Wiccans cast are for personal protection or healing, or they use them to remove negative energies from their environment.

So, being a Wiccan is not so much about performing magick as it is about aligning yourself with the rhythms of Nature and tapping into its endless wisdom and energy.

PART 1

Introduction to Wicca

Chapter 1
What is Wicca?

History of Wicca

Wicca as a new religion first appeared in the early 20th century in the UK. It became a global trend after Gerald Gardner established the Gardnerian Tradition of Wicca, which he based on the book of the witch trials by Margaret Murray.

In other words, Wicca is not a new religion but is a reconstruction of the Nature-based religion followed by different cultures, and in many different ways, for thousands of years until it was replaced by monotheistic religions (Christianity, Judaism, and Islam) about 2,000 years ago.

Fortunately, there are still many cultures whose religious beliefs focus on nature. They worship many gods (e.g., in Hinduism), live according to the rhythms of nature (e.g., indigenous tribes of Siberia and the Amazon), and their religion sees sacred in everything around them (e.g., Taoism, Shinto, etc.). Although the gods they worship and the way they worship them vary, all of these cultures live close to Nature and continuously keep themselves aligned to its rhythms.

The focus of Wicca spirituality is the concept of fertility—life, death, and rebirth—which is why this religion is centered around the Goddess, rather than the God, as is the case with monotheistic religions.

As the fertility of the land depends most of all on the natural elements, Wiccans honor these elements just like Christians honor saints. Therefore, the elements of Earth, Air, Fire, Water, and Spirit, and their associated directions— North, East, South, West, and Center—play a major part in Wicca rituals.

Although witchcraft is part of Wicca (but it doesn't mean all Wiccans are witches), it doesn't include any Satanic rituals. Wicca is about celebrating life in all its forms and does not recognize the concept of "devil." It was monotheistic religions that introduced this idea into religion.

Wicca is not based on rules and dogmas; however, it insists on a strict ethical code of conduct of its members. The Wiccan moral code, or *Wiccan Rede*, is based on the message *Do no harm*.

In other words, you shouldn't join Wicca just to learn to do spells to get back at someone, or to steal someone's husband or job. One thing you should always keep in mind is that whatever energy you send out eventually comes back to you—both positive and negative. So, Wiccans believe that it pays to be kind.

Wiccan rituals are a combination of visualization, mantras, praying, and invocations. Depending on how much time, energy, and resources you want to put into them, they can also include music, drumming, dancing, singing, special clothes and accessories, etc.

Paths and Traditions

There are many forms of Wicca and just as many ways of practicing it, so before you get involved with any particular tradition, try to find out what their core beliefs are. If you decide to join a particular coven, make sure you know what their expectations are. Choose the tradition that you feel most comfortable with. For example, some traditions insist that participants perform rituals naked, so find out as much as you can about the coven you plan to join before you join it.

There are dozens of Wicca traditions and for a novice, this can be confusing. So, until you become more familiar with Wicca practice, learn about the two main traditions on which all other paths were based.

Two main Wicca traditions:

1. Gardnerian Wicca

This tradition was founded by Gerald Gardner, who is known as the father of modern Wicca. This is a formal tradition which requires initiation and works with a degree system. Most of the information passed on to its members is considered secret, and should not to be shared with anyone outside the tradition.

2. Alexandrian Wicca

This tradition was founded by Alex Sanders and is very similar to the Gardnerian Wicca, but it places more emphasis on ceremonial magic during Sabbats and Esbats. It, too, insists on formal initiation of new members and practices a degree system.

These two traditions served as a base from which all other traditions of Wicca were created.

The best known Wiccan paths are:

- British Traditional Wicca (Gardnerian, Alexandrian, Central Valley, Algard, and Blue Star Wicca)
- Eclectic Wicca
- Celtic Wicca
- Saxon Wicca
- Dianic Wicca
- Faery Wicca
- Georgian Wicca
- Odyssean Wicca
- Wiccan Church (which consists of many, to include New Reformed Orthodox Order of the Golden Dawn, Church and School of Wicca, Circle Sanctuary, Covenant of the Goddess, Aquarian Tabernacle Church,

Rowan Tree Church, Covenant of Unitarian Universalists Pagans, and Coven of the Far Flung Net)

Once you decide which path you believe is right for you, you should gradually adopt a Wiccan way of life. The easiest way to do this is to follow the Wheel of the Year calendar and align yourself with the natural cycles it is based on.

Four basic steps to becoming a Wiccan:

1. Develop intuition

Start listening to your inner voice and trusting your instincts. Although this may not be possible in every situation, when you start paying attention to your dreams and your gut feelings, you'll soon realize that life is usually giving you ample warning. The problem is, we usually choose to ignore these hunches.

2. Follow the Wiccan code of ethics

Wiccan Rede is a code of ethics based on the idea that your actions should not harm others. For example, if you're desperate to get a particular job, cast a spell to get this job, but not if it means someone else should get fired for you to get it. Or, if someone is bothering you, you may want to cast a spell so they leave you alone, but not a spell that would kill them.

Besides accepting responsibility for your own thoughts, words, and actions, Wiccan Rede insists that you should also accept responsibility for the consequences of your spells.

3. Start celebrating Sabbats

These are times of the year which mark the changing of the seasons. There are eight Sabbats and you may choose to celebrate all of them, or just one or two. You can make elaborate preparations for these festivals, or you can simply mark the occasion by lighting a candle, leaving some offerings for Mother Earth (e.g., birdseed, or some food for stray or wild animals), and giving thanks.

4. Respect all life

To Wiccans, all life is sacred. Respect this and never do anything that could harm someone or destroy the environment and those whose life depends on it.

Wiccan Rede

Becoming a Wiccan means you agree to live by certain rules.

Wiccan Laws of the craft:

- Witches practice rituals and rites primarily to attune themselves with the natural rhythm of life, and not to do magic, which will alter the reality—theirs or other people's.

- Being able to align themselves with this rhythm of nature gives witches a responsibility toward the environment. They seek to live in harmony with Nature and protect it. So, in a way, witches were our first environmental activists. This is in complete contrast to the anthropocentrism of the Biblical traditions that assumes human superiority over nature.

- Witches believe that supernatural power is within the reach of those who know and want to tap into it.

- Witches believe in harmony, and this includes the divinity. They believe that both genders have to be present during rituals, which is why they summon both the Goddess and her consort, the God. Sex is a normal part of life, always has been and always will be, so this is nothing to be ashamed of or feel guilty about.

- Witches recognize the existence of both the physical and spiritual world. Magic happens when you learn how to successfully interact between the two.

- Although some covens do have High Priestesses, generally speaking, witches do not recognize any authoritarian hierarchy. However, they do honor those who teach and share their knowledge and wisdom.

- For witches, magic is part of life and witchcraft is the Wiccan way.

- You cannot inherit the position of a witch from a family member—you have to become a witch in your own right. However, just by calling yourself a witch does not make you one. You become one through knowledge and skill of witchcraft.

- Witches do not recognize the concept of absolute evil; entities known as Satan or the Devil are part of Christian dogma. However, witches believe in negative forces and energies which they dispel with the help of banishing ritual magic.

- Witches honor Nature and believe that everything we need for our health and wellbeing can be found there.

- The Goddess manifests in three forms as a Maiden, Mother, and Crone.

- Each Goddess has a consort, or as some call him, a husband.

- That as long as you harm no one, you can do what you like. This is the law.

- Witches are bound by the Threefold Law: whatever you create, be it laughter or pain, joy or sorrow, is returned to you threefold.

- Witches seek to live in harmony, not only with each other but with the Earth, that which is our womb and our home.

- That death is NOT the end of existence, but a step in the ongoing circle of life.

- That there is NO sacrifice of blood, for she is the mother of all living things and from all things proceed unto her, and unto her, all things return. Killing is for survival and defense only.

- Wiccans do not seek converts. The Way is open to those who, for whatever reason, seek and find the craft.

Chapter 2
Wiccan Beliefs

Gods and Goddesses

In Wicca, the Goddess, Mother Earth, is the key divinity, and although many Wiccans worship only the Goddess, most believe in duality of worship. This means that during rituals they also invoke the masculine aspect of divinity. We can learn a lot about ancient Pagan religion by observing Hinduism, which is the oldest surviving polytheistic religion. In Hinduism, every Goddess has a consort, and we assume the same was true in all pre-Christianity religions.

As Wicca is about living in harmony, invoking both the Goddess and the God is also about maintaining balance in nature (and in our own lives). Besides, we all possess both masculine and feminine qualities, so when you honor deities of both genders, you are honoring both sides of yourself.

Summoning the Goddess and the God is how you start a ritual. You cast a circle and mark the four cardinal quarters and then summon the deity you want to be present, such as the deity you hope to get help or guidance from. The presence of a deity is very important because when a deity is present, the circle you had cast automatically becomes a sacred space.

Focusing their religion on Goddess (the female aspect) is how our ancestors honored life, (the miracle of birth and rebirth). We know this from thousands of female figurines discovered by archaeologists throughout Europe. What this shows is that for most of human history, until about 2,000 years ago, a female deity was seen as a more powerful and important one and it was only with the arrival of patriarchal Indo-European tribes from Asia that the focus of worship shifted from the Moon and Goddess, to the Sun and God.

Wicca, just like other polytheistic religions, is about worshipping many gods so you don't have to focus on one deity, but can choose several you feel attracted to or those you feel would best match your intent.

In other words, you can invoke the same Goddess every time you cast a spell, or you can summon different deities for different occasions. For example, you will invoke one Goddess when praying for a child, and another one when praying to succeed in a job interview. Still, if you feel particularly close to a certain deity, it is perfectly all right to invoke that deity regardless of the intent.

Besides, many Wiccans only feel comfortable with deities from their own culture. A German may find it easier to invoke a Norse deity than an Egyptian one, a Russian may feel closer to a Slavic deity than a Celtic one, etc.

However, as religion is a very personal experience, regardless of where you're from and where you live, it's best to choose a deity you feel most comfortable with and can easily relate to.

So, before you get into Wicca, perhaps you should do some research and learn about various ancient religions (Norse, Celtic, ancient Greek and Roman, Egyptian, Mesopotamian, Hindu, Chinese, etc.) and what their chief deities were. You can easily find all the information you need on the Internet.

How to Use Elements in Rituals

Wiccans experience the world through the four Elements, which actually represent the four qualities present in all of us and in the world around us. Just like in Ayurveda, these elements have their physical and metaphysical aspects.

Four Elements Wiccans invoke in their rituals:

- Air
- Water
- Earth
- Fire

From the physical point of view, Elements are what we are surrounded with and each one of them is essential for our survival. We need air to breath, water represents 70% of our body mass, Earth is what we walk on and grow our crops on, and fire keeps us warm and helps us prepare our meals.

On the other hand, the metaphysical interpretation of these elements is about what we are like as individuals. For example, fire makes you warm and passionate, but also short-tempered and aggressive. Air is good for your intellect and helps you communicate easily, but too much air can make you pompous or scattered. Earth can make you realistic and grounded, but too much of it can make you too rigid in your views and stubborn. Water boosts your creativity and imagination, but too much of it can make you naive and a dreamer.

As in Wicca rituals, intent is represented by symbols, so it's clear why the five Elements play such an important role in Wicca magic.

The power of intention is crucial in spellcasting, because the more powerful the intention, the more successful the spell. Concentration is key, and while some people can stay focused on one thing for hours at a time, others will struggle to concentrate even for ten minutes. If this is you, perhaps you should first learn how to improve your concentration and then move on to spellwork.

Four things that help you stay focused during a ritual:

1. Clear goals

One of the reasons spells often don't work is that they are not cast properly. It's not enough to say "I want a job" or "I want to meet my soulmate."

Spells need to be very specific: You should indicate what kind of a job you'd like, or what kind of a person you'd like to meet—but this is where it gets difficult because we often don't really know what we want. When you spell out what exactly you want help with, or when you force yourself to write it down, you are making yourself think about your wish strategically. And once you know exactly what it is you need, finding it becomes much easier.

2. Composure

Spellcasting requires your full concentration and can be energy-consuming especially if rituals last for hours, as they sometimes do. This is why you should never try to cast a spell if you feel exhausted, depressed, or angry because these emotions can be very energy-draining, so you will have not enough left for the ritual itself. If you can't postpone the ritual for another time, have a glass of water or a cup of tea and sit quietly for twenty minutes until you feel more grounded and composed.

3. Patience

Even when done properly, some spells take longer to manifest. To improve your chances of your wish coming true, be prepared to repeat rituals consistently for as long as it takes. It's unrealistic to expect a miracle overnight.

4. Direction

Spellcasting is about using your mental energy to change yours or somebody else's reality. To make it easier for your thoughts to be channeled where they need to go, you have to help yourself stay focused during the ritual. Therefore, think carefully about what you'd like the outcome of the ritual to be, what elements and deities need to be invoked, what mantras or chants need to be said, how your altar needs to be arranged, what tools you'll need, etc. Go through all of this in your head BEFORE you step into the Circle, so you don't realize halfway through the ritual you forgot to buy a candle.

The main reason we invoke elements in a ritual is to help us stay focused on what we are doing. For example, if you are dealing with love issues, focusing on the element of fire—on the symbols representing it such as a candle, items in red color, images of a happy couple, etc.—will help you channel your energy where you want it to go.

However, magic doesn't happen only during spellcasting. By simply keeping symbols of certain elements near you (e.g., carrying a piece of amethyst in your pocket to help you deal with stress, wearing a rose quartz pendant when searching for love, etc.), you are keeping yourself aligned with your intent even when you are not casting a spell.

If the size of your altar allows it, you can keep symbols of all the elements displayed on your altar all the time, or you can display only those your latest spell focused on. You can also wear the symbols of certain elements on your person (as jewelry), keep them in your desk, or carry them in your bag.

The Wheel of the Year

Those who belong to cultures that are still close to nature, times when the seasons change are probably the most important times of the year, because when seasons change, everything changes.

In ancient times, when people often lived at the mercy of the elements, seasonal changes played a major role in their lives. As the length of the day changes with the seasons, and the Sun decides how long a day will be, it is not surprising that most early civilizations worshipped the Sun.

For example, ancient Egyptians worshipped hundreds of gods, but the chief deity was the Sun god Amon-Ra. Zoroastrians worshipped the fire because it, just like the Sun, provided light and warmth, for example.

We live at a time when we are usually cushioned from the elements and the whims of nature, but Wiccans still respect these times and most of their seasonal festivals are celebrated on or around the summer or winter solstice, or spring and autumn equinox.

Veneration of the Sun takes many forms, and is still widely celebrated throughout the world, although often in disguise. Many of the festivals of the dominant religions are nothing more than disguised ancient Pagan celebrations of arrival of spring (Easter), winter (Christmas), Wicca New Year (All Souls Day), etc.

It is these festivals that make up the Wheel of the Year. They are called Sabbats.

From the scientific point of view, there is a reason why these times were so important not just for early man, but until about 100 years ago, for all farmers. The Wheel of the Year is nothing more than a division of a year into four seasons, each one of which is the time for a certain kind of work on the land. Besides, these four seasons mark the never-ending cycle of birth, growth, death, and rebirth that those living close to land are constantly reminded of.

So what happens during a Sabbat celebration? There is usually a ritual focusing on certain aspects of the Goddess (depending on the Sabbat that is being celebrated), followed by a feast and merrymaking.

Although there are many ways of celebrating Sabbats, of which often depend on the Wicca tradition a particular coven is following, generally speaking, the Spring and Summer Sabbats focus on fertility and abundance, while Autumnal and Winter Sabbats revolve around the harvest and weakening of the Sun.

Observing the Wheel of the Year calendar is about paying attention to the seasonal changes taking place around you and making sure your own life is aligned to these changes. For example, Winter is the time when nature dies down so you should spend more time indoors resting, regenerating, and if possible, doing some inner work. Summer solstice, on the other hand, when the Sun is at its strongest, is a powerful time for spells to boost your health or wealth. During the Spring equinox, when the day and night are of equal length, you can cast spells for inner balance, or if you feel energized by the season of new beginning, you can plan new projects. In Autumn, you consider everything you've achieved so far and give thanks for what you have.

Sabbats and Esbats

Sabbats

We know Pagan cultures observed eight of these ancient festivals, or Sabbats, although not all cultures celebrated all of them, nor were they celebrated at the same time, or in the same manner.

Wicca divides the Sabbats into two group of festivals:

- **The Fire Festivals (or cross-quarter festivals)**

These include Imbolc, Beltane, Lammas, and Samhain. Cross quarter days fall halfway between an equinox and solstice.

- **The Solar Festivals (or quarter festivals)**

These are two solstices (Litha and Yule), and two equinoxes (Ostara and Mabon).

Four Fire Festivals:

1) **Imbolc**

Imbolc was celebrated on the February 1st and 2nd, but Christians turned this celebration into St.

Brighid's Day or Candlemas. In February, days start getting longer, so this festival marks the end of winter and the beginning of spring. The Imbolc celebrations focus on the strengthening of the Sun.

2) **Beltane**

Beltane marked the beginning of Summer. It took place in early May and is now replaced by the May 1st holiday. This is the time of spring rains and greening of the earth, and Beltane celebrations focus on the fertility of Nature.

3) **Lughnasadh/Lammas**

This festival marked the time of the first harvest and took place on August 1st and 2nd. This was a time of major thanksgiving celebrations. There are still many local festivals celebrated at this time. Traditionally, people prayed and offered sacrifice for the success of future crops, and symbolically what you've achieved by Lammas is your main achievement for the year.

4) **Samhain**

This festival was known as the witches' New Year, so, in a way, this is a time when you have a chance to turn a new leaf.

Samhain is also the time to remember the dead. This is believed to be a magical time when the veil between the world of the dead and the living is thin and when contacting the dead is easy. In rituals performed at this time one must honor, remember, and speak of the dead. Christianity replaced Samhain with the All Soul's Day festival.

Spiritually, winter is a time for turning inwards, for reflecting both on the summer behind us and the spring ahead of us.

Four Solar Festivals:

1. **Winter Solstice (Yule) – December 20/21**

This marks the shortest day of the year. The focus of this Sabbat is the return of the Sun, as the winter solstice days become longer by approximately two minutes a day.

In terms of spellwork, winter is considered a good time for grounding and inner work, as well as for banishing spells.

2. Spring Equinox (Ostara) – March 21/22

On this day, Wiccans celebrate the arrival of Spring and the focus of this Sabbat is on new life. This is the time of the year when hours of light and darkness are equal, so you can do spells for inner balance.

3. Summer Solstice (Litha) – June 21/22

This festival marks the longest day of the year and is also known as Midsummer. The Sun is at its strongest so the Litha rituals are about abundance. You can use the energy of the Sun and do spells to boost your health, financial situation, or love life.

4. Autumn Equinox (Mabon) – September 21/22

This is another time of the year when hours of light and darkness are equal. Symbolically, Mabon is the time of giving thanks for everything you have, such as health, family, friends, employment, etc.

Some traditions of Wicca celebrate only Fire festivals, while others observe only Solar festivals.

Celebrating all eight Sabbats can be impractical, so choose the ones you feel most drawn to.

Esbats

Esbats are the festivals celebrated on the thirteen full moons that occur every year. As most nature-based religions center their spirituality around the Goddess, the Moon is much more important to these religions than the Sun.

Not only do different Moon phases affect us in different ways, they can also be used to symbolically mark different stages of a woman's life. However, the Full Moon is believed to be the time when the Goddess magic is stronger than at any other time of the month, so the most important spells should be performed during this phase, ideally in the open.

We know from archaeological records that people have celebrated the Midwinter (Yule) for about 12,000 years. However, we also know that lunar calendar dates were observed as long ago as 30,000 BC. Bones, antlers, stones, and goddess figures marked with periodic notches carved into it found throughout Europe took a long time to be deciphered, but eventually scientists agreed that they represent a crude calendar.

These were probably the first attempts at keeping record of lunar phases. The mysterious thirteen lines are now believed to indicate the thirteen days from the visible New Moon to the Full Moon, or the thirteen New Moons of each yearly cycle.

However, there are many other reasons why the Moon played, and still plays, an important role in the life of our planet. It causes the tides, it affects the speed of Earth's rotation and thus affects the climate, it stabilizes the planet's poles without which climate would be absolutely unpredictable, etc.

Besides, the Moon is our closest celestial neighbor and is hard to be ignored. Those who spend a lot of time outdoors know that there is something hypnotizing about gazing at the Full Moon, which may be why Wicca covens traditionally meet on the Full Moon or the New Moon days. As a solitary practitioner you can celebrate both, or just one.

Early man was very observant of his environment and compared the three phases of the Moon—Waxing, Full, and Waning Moon—with the three cycles of life—birth, growth, and death.

Moon phases and three stages of a woman's life:

- **The Waxing phase** (when the moon is growing) symbolically represents a strong, independent young woman who knows what she wants in life and how to get it. This phase is about birth and growth.

- **The Full Moon** symbolizes the mother aspect and is about fertility, nourishment, and protection of life.

- **The Waning Moon** represents the aged and wise crone aspect, a symbol of maturity, wisdom, intuition, and healing.

Different phases of the Moon have different energy and symbolism and Wiccans align with these phases in order to make the most of these specific energies and use them to empower their spells:

- **New Moon**

The energy of this phase is used for personal growth, healing, and blessing. During the New Moon phase it's best to do spells to boost the beginning of a relationship or a project, to create something new, or bless a new arrival (e.g., a baby, a car, a new home, etc.).

- **Waxing Moon**

The energy of this phase is good for attracting something (e.g., love, health, protection). It's a good time to do spells concerning growth of a business, love, friendship, etc.

- **Full Moon**

This is a very powerful time to draw on the energy of the Moon to deal with major problems, decisions, or personal crisis. Reserve the days of the Full Moon for spells that are really important for you, when you know you will need a major boost for anything you do. Don't waste the Full Moon day's energy on minor issues.

- **Waning Moon**

This phase is good for banishing and rejecting emotions, situations, and people that affect you negatively. In other words, get rid of whatever is no longer serving you.

- **Dark Moon**

This is the period of three days prior to the New Moon. Traditionally, no magic is performed at this time, but this is a good time for meditation and contemplation.

Chapter 3
Other Beliefs

Reincarnation

Reincarnation is the philosophical concept that a living being can start a new life in a different physical body after its biological death. This process is also referred to as rebirth and is central to many religions, such as Hinduism, Jainism, Buddhism, and Sikhism. The followers of these religions believe that after death, the mind continues to exist by moving on to the next life.

According to this philosophy, it's wrong to try and end suffering (physical or emotional) by committing suicide because if the mind lives on after death, it simply means that killing yourself will not be the end to your suffering. After your physical death, your mind will simply take on another form and you will, as a new person, continue to suffer. Therefore, deal with the problem—don't try to run away from it.

No one knows for sure what happens when we die, but according to religions who believe in reincarnation, when the heart stops, we enter a dream-like state that is typical of time between death and rebirth. After a few days or weeks, this state ends and we are born as a different person without ever remembering our previous life.

It's believed that by observing one's nature and personality, it's easy to guess what they could have been in their previous lives. Many believe that it's surprisingly easy to spot typical character traits of very young children and predict what their character is going to be like. From a very early age, children are either good-natured, empathic, and kind, or prone to cruelty, bullying, envy, and selfishness.

The fact that children from the same family (even twins) often exhibit extreme differences in character, despite having the same parents, it is believed to be the sign of what they were in previous lives.

Those who believe in reincarnation claim that mental tendencies are developed through repeated actions over a long period of time. So, if a child of four exhibits clear signs of bullying, it is obvious that he must have developed those traits in his previous life, for it is too young to have had time to develop them in this life. In other words, a child's current values and behaviors are a sign of who and what they were in the previous life.

Is it possible to know if you have reincarnated? Although this is impossible to prove, there are certain signs that may indicate that your soul may have experienced different lifetimes.

<u>Nine signs your soul may have reincarnated:</u>

1. If you feel passionately for or against something and you are not sure why you feel that way.

2. If you easily learned a particular foreign language and speak it fluently, this could have been your mother tongue in your previous life.

3. If you keep on having the same dream over and over again, it is always about the same country (or a place), and you always die in your dream.

4. If you are considered "wise beyond your years," it is often a sign of accumulated knowledge and wisdom from your past lives.

5. If a child has weird memories that others know they did not experience (in this life).

6. If you have a *deja vu* feeling about a certain place, although you've never been there before.

7. If you feel drawn to a particular period of time, or to a certain culture or a way of life, and you have no idea why.

8. If you have fears that you can't explain.

9. If you don't feel at home in this world.

The Afterlife

We all know what happens to our body when we die, but no one knows what happens to our consciousness.

The concept of afterlife is the belief that an individual's consciousness continues to exist after the death of the physical body. This concept is addressed in different ways by different religions.

In 2010, a well-known regenerative medicine scientist, Robert Lanza, came up with a theory that our consciousness does not die with us, but moves on. According to Lanza, if the body generates consciousness, then consciousness dies when the body dies. But new studies suggest that if the body receives consciousness in the same way that a TV set receives satellite signals, that means that consciousness does not end at the death of the physical body.

There are many documented cases of individuals who were clinically dead (showing no brain activity), who remember everything that was happening to them on the medical table at the time when they were clinically dead.

Unfortunately, modern science believes only in what can be proven in a lab.

All religions based on Abrahamic tradition claim that the dead go to a place (either a heaven or a hell) from which they cannot return. Where they will go is decided by God. On the other hand, religions which believe in reincarnation believe that how many times a person will be reborn depends on their actions, rather than by somebody else's decision.

Animism

To fully understand Wicca, you have to understand the concept of animism.

Animistic beliefs are based on the idea that everything that exists in the Universe has some kind of energy that makes them alive and gives them a certain kind of consciousness, such as with trees, animals, rivers, stars, etc.

There are still societies where animism is the way of life and by studying those cultures we can gain an insight into what animistic religions of early civilizations were like. Comparative studies of Shinto, Hinduism, Taoism, and indigenous cultures of Siberia, Africa, and South America help us guess how Pagan religions developed and how they were practiced.

To early man, there was no difference between the living and non-living worlds and this is why they treated all animals, plants, and natural elements with respect and reverence.

As hunters depended on animals for survival, they continuously performed rituals to give thanks to the animals that allowed themselves to be killed and provide food. They not only honored the animals they killed for food, but also the rain and sun which provided food and water for the animals they hunted.

Even when they settled down and became farmers, people were still at the mercy of nature, and flooding or droughts often meant the difference between life and death. This is why man continuously tried to win the favors of the spirits that provided life-giving rain and kept death and disease away from their communities.

For a similar reason, the early man paid a lot of respect to their dead. They believed that the spirits of the dead could be a source of protection and guidance, but also a source of accidents and bad luck, so they took great care to bury the dead with due respect and to placate their spirits by offering gifts.

It was feared that improper burial ceremonies would make the dead refuse to leave the earth and instead remain stuck in the community they had come from, causing accidents and bad luck.

For this reason, great effort was put into ensuring the dead were buried in a way that would guarantee they would leave the earth for good.

Ancestor worship can be observed in most formal religions of today, as the burial customs and religious festivals are simply remnants of pagan ancestor worship ceremonies.

Perhaps the best example of this is the most important Sabbat in Wicca religion, the Samhain, celebrated on October 31st. We know that as Christianity spread across Europe and became the dominant religion, many Pagan festivals took on Christian names and guises.

Today, two major Christian festivals commemorating the dead—All Saints' Day (celebrated on November 1st in honor of Christian saints and martyrs) and All Souls' Day (celebrated on November 2nd in honor of the souls of the dead)—are celebrated at the same time as Samhain. Coincidence? I don't think so.

PART 2

Introduction to Witchcraft

Chapter 4
What is Witchcraft?

Witches and Witchcraft

The term "witch" comes from the Anglo-Saxon word "wicca," meaning "wise." Witches, therefore, are the "wise" women and witchcraft is the "craft of the wise." Although the term "witch" is often misunderstood, it usually refers to someone who possesses magical powers, who practice sorcery, and who communes with spirits and deities.

During the witch hunt of the Middle Ages, tens of thousands of these wise women were killed at the stake throughout Western Europe where the Catholic Church felt threatened by this female power. One can only imagine how much esoteric knowledge was lost because of this carnage.

Together with the wise women, hundreds of thousands of cats were killed as well, for they were believed to be part of witchcraft. Science has, in the meantime, found that such massive destruction of cats in Western Europe during the Middle Ages may have been the reason the plague spread so fast, killing millions of people across the continent. The bubonic plague was caused by infected fleas and lice which lived on rats, and with no cats to get rid of them, the plague spread like fire.

It is also believed that one of the reasons the Catholic church felt threatened by Paganism was that in Pagan traditions, men and women are seen as equal. That was against the core beliefs of the Church, which saw women as inferior in relation to men, and who therefore perceived these beliefs as a real threat to the Patriarchal system. Therefore, the witch hunt was also the war against the power of women.

The Wiccan movement is growing fast mainly because people now have a better understanding of what Wicca is about, but also because of the more tolerant social climate where many Wiccans feel it's safe to "come out."

Three reasons for the increased popularity of Wicca:

- "Green" living and care for the environment have become a popular trend that touches on many aspects of our life, such as diet, fitness, alternative healing methods, wildlife conservation, eco-packaging, recycling, minimalist living practices, etc. Wicca as a nature-based religion fits in nicely.

- Most Pagan religions, including Wicca, promote gender equality—and as our society has become much more tolerant in this respect than it was fifty years ago, it is not surprising that more and more people identify themselves with a religion where they feel accepted.

- Social media has helped spread the information about what Wicca really is about, as well as what it is NOT about. It is ridiculous that the Church points a finger at Wicca and blames Wiccans for being a Satanic cult, when it was Christianity and other monotheistic religions that introduced the concept of

Devil and Hell into religion. Besides, Wiccans are not magicians and the magic they perform has to do with one's own energy.

Wiccan Tools

Wiccan tools are essential for rituals and spellcasting and can range from a single piece of crystal to an altar full of various items and symbols, as well as special clothes, headdress, and jewelry.

Although you will need certain tools to perform a ritual, what's much more important for the spell to work is the power of your intent. In themselves, tools do not possess magic, but they do possess the power to change your subconscious by creating a certain atmosphere in which you can relax enough and focus sufficiently on your intent. It is the power of this intent that makes the spell work or not. Therefore, tools are simply mediums which help you switch off and become open to the world of spirit, which indirectly make spells successful or not.

For this reason, Wiccan tools are both very personal and potentially very powerful things that you can create magic with. This is why items you find and feel drawn to, like feathers, unusual pieces of wood, leaves, etc., are much more efficient than expensive and beautifully-designed items you can buy in specialized Wicca shops. However, as your Wiccan tools allow you access to the world of spirit, you should treat them with respect.

Items displayed on the altar can range from very expensive ones you buy from specialized shops to simple items you find in your home or garden. What's important is that regardless of how simple or sophisticated they are, they have a special meaning to YOU. An altar is a sacred place, in front of which you will pray, chant, contact the dead, or enter into an altered state of consciousness, so it should consist of ritual tools which are charged by yourself and which work for you.

Wiccan tools should never be lent or borrowed or even touched by others, as handling them makes it possible for others' negative energy to be passed onto your tools. This is particularly true of crystals. However, if this happens, cleanse and recharge your tools before using them again.

How to look after your ritual tools:

- Keep them clean
- Charge them occasionally
- Keep them away from sunlight when not using them
- Don't let others touch them
- Keep them wrapped in a cloth, or individually in case of crystals, when not using them

So, which tools to keep on your altar? This depends on what you hope to achieve, and you may need different tools for different rituals. However, all the Wiccan tools you buy or get from someone have to be cleansed and charged as soon as you get home. This will free them of any negative energy they might have picked up while they were on display or while they belonged to someone else.

The basic Wiccan tools are:

Altar

Ideally, altars should be kept in a room used only for rituals, but very few people can afford that. Instead, choose a corner of the room you spend the most time in. You can place it on a table, coffee table, windowsill, mantlepiece, on the floor, or even inside a drawer. Choose a place where you'll be able to easily reach the displayed objects and where they will not be seen or touched by others.

You can set up a permanent altar, or create one only when you want to cast a spell or celebrate Sabbat.

A permanent altar is usually placed somewhere where you will often see it, and it should contain items which symbolize the four elements, plus anything else you'd like to keep there.

When setting up the altar for a special occasion, you will use items symbolic of the intent you are casting the spell for. For example, if casting a love spell, you will focus on the Fire element and use symbols and colors that boost that particular element (e.g., rose quartz crystal, red candles, etc.). For a job spell, you will focus on the Earth element and use symbols and colors which support it (e.g., green, brown, or dark yellow colors, coins, images of gold, etc.).

As it's difficult to keep all your tools and items on display all the time, it's best to keep only a few items on permanent display and add new ones once you know what you're casting a spell for.

Athame

This is a ceremonial knife which is the main ritual tool in Wicca. Its main purpose is to channel and direct psychic energy during a ritual. You can use it when casting a Circle and should never use it for cutting (you can use an ordinary knife for that purpose).

Pentacle

This is a flat disk in the shape of the five-pointed star, usually made of metal or wood. Some Wiccans hang it over doors and windows for protection but it can also be used to invoke spirits.

Candles

Candle color should match the energy you are trying to invoke (e.g., red for passion, blue for calm, brown for money matters, etc.), although white ones can always be used as a substitute.

Candles represent the Fire and Air elements and are essential for all rituals. It's best to use candles made of natural wax and ideally, you should have a collection of white, black, green, red, yellow, blue, gold, and silver candles. It's best to get medium or small candles, for in most rituals you have to wait for a candle to burn down before you can close a Circle, and with a big one, this can take hours.

Crystals

Crystals are essential for many rituals because they are great conductors of energy, however, because they so easily absorb energy from the environment, they have to be regularly cleansed and charged. Don't let others touch them, and if you use them in spellwork involving other people, make sure you cleanse and recharge them after the ritual.

The Wand

The wand is used for casting a circle, although you can also use the athame or your own hand with a pointed forefinger. Wands are usually made of wood because wood is an excellent conductor of energy and magic.

Bells

The main purpose of bells in rituals is to create or raise vibrations.

Drums & Rattles

Drumming and shaking a rattle is usually done as part of the cleansing ceremony when someone's aura or a certain space needs to be rid of negative energy. Drums and rattles are often used in house-cleansing ceremonies in order to free them of the previous occupants' energies.

Herbs & Essential Oil

Essential oils are usually used for anointing candles, while herbs can be burned instead of incense or used to mark the Circle boundary.

Treat your Wiccan tools with respect. Charge them to align them with your own energy, so they are happy to "work" for you.

Chapter 5
Ritual and Spellwork

Why We Do Rituals

Rituals are the essence of Wicca and they may be very simple, involving just a few gestures, words, and objects—or complex and sophisticated and take several hours to complete.

Our everyday life is full of small rituals, although we are usually not even aware of them. On the other hand, in ancient societies, and in some cultures even today, life revolved around endless rituals, or *rites*, which were performed every day or several times a day. The purpose of these ceremonies was to appease the gods or spirits of the deceased and ensure good luck in hunt, protection of one's family or property, or boost the fertility of the land or animals, for example.

Generally speaking, rituals are certain actions which enable us to escape the mundane and step into the world of the spirit. But the trick with rituals is that they have to be performed on a regular basis because it is the consistency of repetitive action that gives those actions a meaning.

When it comes to Wicca rituals, repetition of certain steps during a ritual eventually makes the ritual performance your second nature. For example, if you use a blue candle to promote healing, tranquility, and peaceful sleep, over time you will require less and less concentration and effort while performing this particular spell because the meaning of the color blue in your mind will be associated with health, peace of mind, and relaxation.

A ritual repeated numerous times makes it easier to not only perform it, because you don't have to think about details, but it also helps you slip into another reality more quickly. This is particularly important for solitary witches who perform rituals on their own, and this is why it is recommended that once you work out how to cast a Circle, invoke deities, or align the Elements to your goal, stick to it until the process becomes your second nature. Otherwise, if you keep on changing the way you perform rituals, it becomes like reinventing the wheel. For example, opening and closing rituals should be the same every time.

Therefore, the success of a ritual and the ease with which it is performed depend on the consistency of the performance.

Six basic steps to follow when performing a ritual:

1. Purification

Both the place where the ritual will take place and the person performing it should be clean. This can take the form of a ritual bath, a smudging ceremony (with sage, rosemary, or lavender), and drumming or clapping hands to remove any negative energy that might be lurking in the ritual space.

2. Setting up the altar

You may keep a permanent altar or set one up one for each ritual, but chances are you will need different items for different occasions so it's best to set up an altar once you know what spell you'll be casting.

3. Casting a Circle

By doing this you create a boundary between the mundane and the sacred world. You may mark the boundary with sea salt, stones, herbs, candles, or by an imaginary border you draw with your wand through the air.

4. Invocation

Invoke the deities and the Elements you want to work with. Elements and colors carry different energies, which you should try and match to what you want your ritual to achieve (e.g., Water for inner-balance and creativity, Fire for passion and energy, Air for communication and legal matters, Earth for stability and money-related issues).

5. The ritual begins

This is the main part of the ritual and should revolve around stating the intent, communicating with your deities, and performing the ritual itself. The ritual may include the reading of ancient mystical texts, one's own poetry written for the occasion, performing a drama, saying prayers, etc. There are no rules and you can do anything you feel is right for the occasion.

6. Closing the ritual

Opening and closing the ritual should always be the same and should include extinguishing the candles that have not burned down and giving thanks.

However, before you get involved with spellwork, especially if you plan to do them for others, make sure you understand what Wicca is about and what you may be getting yourself into if you decide to do black magic. Besides, it's best not to perform rituals for others until you have gained sufficient experience with spellwork. However, once you start casing spells for others, respect their privacy.

If you do a particular spell repeatedly and it doesn't work, perhaps the Universe has a reason for not granting you your wish right now, or maybe you need to be patient as some spells take longer to manifest, or maybe you need to use a different spell.

Generally speaking, spells are divided into white magic and black magic spells. Wicca is about not doing harm to others, so be very careful if you want to start experimenting with black magic.

White magic spells are typically blessing and healing spells, while black magic spells focus on causing harm to others, (e.g., bad luck spell, guilt spell, nightmare hex, etc.). Regardless of how much someone may deserve to be punished for what they have done, remember that spells DO work, so if you decide to try any of these, make sure you can live with the consequences and events these spells could trigger.

The reason spells DO work is that while preparing them and while performing them, you force yourself to focus on the issue you are addressing, and sometimes, all it takes for someone to heal or find a solution to a problem is to focus on the issue and channel their personal energy in the right direction.

The Power of Magic: Healing, Revenge, Curses

Magic is the art of changing reality according to one's Will. However, it's not as simple as casting a spell and expecting to get what you want. The reason many people have a problem with magic is that it is not always ethical and may accidentally affect someone else in your environment. It's well-known that spells and talismans one carries for protection, or to draw something into one's life, can "leak" into someone else's life.

Four things to consider before performing magic:

1. **Is magic ethical?**

Would you cast a spell for someone who wanted someone else dead? According to Wiccan Rede, you can do any kind of magic, as long as it does no harm. What's "harmful" is relative and the bottom line is that magic in itself is not good or bad—it is your intention that makes it such. Magic is simply a tool and the way you use it will make it white, black, or grey.

On the other hand, if someone who is a well-known criminal, pedophile, or woman abuser asks you to help him heal, would you do it? Would you help him heal even if you know he will continue to destroy people's lives?

If you plan to do magic spells for others, this is something you have to be clear about before you start seeing clients.

2. Make it happen

For a spell to work, a lot of energy has to be put into it. Whatever it is you desire, a lifelong partner, a high-profile job, or a beautiful body, you have to work for it. It's not enough to cast a spell and expect a miracle.

For example, regardless of how powerful certain spells may be, you are unlikely to find a partner if you neglect yourself, stay at home all the time, or have unrealistic expectations. Also, no magic can help you have a beautiful body if you eat junk food, smoke, or eat throughout the day. So, spells DO work but you have to fulfill your part of the bargain too.

3. Leaking spells

There are cases when someone carries a talisman to get pregnant, but does nothing else about it, and is angry to find out that a colleague sitting next to her actually got pregnant (whether she wanted to or not is another question).

Or you wear a talisman to win a lottery, but often forget to buy the lotto ticket and are furious when you find out that your brother won the lottery (even though he didn't carry a talisman or had a spell cast for this purpose). In other words, the Universe will do its part to make the magic happen but you have to do yours too. Just like you won't get a job unless you keep on applying for one, and you won't find new love if you stay at home waiting to be discovered, you have to help magic work for you.

In other words, a spell cast for you, or a talisman you wear for a particular reason, will work; it may not work for YOU, but for someone else you are physically or mentally close with.

4. **Be grateful**

Although magic is supposed to make everything possible, it's important to be realistic when demanding something. For example, if you dream and repeatedly cast a spell to win $1 million, and you get only $100,000, remember that it's not always possible to get what you want when you want it, so be grateful for what you did get. Also, it doesn't mean you will not get the million you dream of sometime in the future, so continue to "feed" your dream, because both dreams and magic need the energy to keep them alive.

So, how does magic actually work? It probably has something to do with the earth's electromagnetic field (EM) that some people are sensitive to. EM affects us in many ways, although with most people the ability to pick up these vibrations has been lost or has become dormant.

Numerous scientific studies show that meditation, visualization, and prayer affect our subconscious and indirectly transform our psyche. Perhaps magic works in a similar way.

The energy that powers magic, (i.e., that transforms your intent into reality), is very real and happens all the time. That energy is your intent. For your intent to manifest into something tangible, you have to feed it with fire (i.e., you have to feel real passion about what you are trying to achieve with your spell).

But how the Universe transforms your intent into reality is something no one has been able to explain so far. However, the passion behind your spell—the pain, rage, love, or hope you project when you cast a spell—is often all the Universe needs to make your wish come true.

Casting a Circle

Rituals and spells are essential to Wicca. They are performed within a Circle which, once cast, becomes a sacred space because it symbolically defines a boundary of a place where you face your deities, where you may enter the altered state of consciousness, and where the magic happens. You keep the boundaries of this space "protected" by the symbols of the elements and the deities you decide to invoke during the ritual.

Before casting a circle, prepare the space where the ritual will take place by cleaning it and clearing it of clutter. Make sure you are not be disturbed for at least thirty minutes, otherwise there's not much point in casting a Circle. Switch off your phone, take your pets out of the room, and don't answer the doorbell.

To cast a circle and perform magic (for yourself or others), you have to become a conduit for the energy that is created within the Circle. Different techniques work for different people, but the easiest way to prepare yourself for this is to take a few minutes to relax, take a few slow breaths, and slowly open up your energy points.

You can also raise your power by energizing your body through dancing, clapping your hands, drumming, singing, etc. Do this for about ten minutes, then shake your arms and legs to ground yourself.

When you are ready, draw as much energy as you can to your arm holding the athame with which you will cast a Circle. If you don't have the athame, you can use a wand, a branch, or a finger instead to draw a line in the air marking the boundary of your ritual space.

Start by marking the four cardinal points of the Circle (north, south, east, and west) by objects that symbolically represent each of the Elements.

For example, Earth is in the north and you can mark it with something that represents the Element of earth, such as a piece of rock, a crystal, etc. Water is in the West so in the West you can place something that stands for water, like a small dish of water, a picture of a lake, or a blue piece of cloth. Do this for all four cardinal points.

Once you have cast a Circle, ask for the presence of a deity you want to work with. This can be a Goddess you feel particularly drawn to, or a deity known to help with particular issues to include love, healing, fortune, etc.

At the end of each ritual, don't forget to thank the deities and elementals you had invoked, then close the Circle. As spellcasting can be emotionally draining, have a glass of water and sit quietly for a few moments to ground yourself.

Setting Up an Altar

For Wiccans, the altar is a sacred space where they meditate, visualize, cast spells, perform rituals, and commune with their deities.

If you are new to Wicca, the first thing you should do is create an altar, which will serve as a starting point for everything else you do in Wicca.

Your altar should always be clean and vibrant, for dust and clutter prevent energy from flowing smoothly. Decorate it with meaningful things which symbolize the four elements, the deities you work with, the seasons, etc.

Whatever items you decide to keep on your altar, the items placed there should represent your own values and beliefs. Therefore, rather than buy expensive tools, use what you have or create items that are meaningful to you and that represent who you are.

Things to consider when creating an altar:

1. Indoor vs outdoor altar

Traditionally, Pagans worship under the sky and Nature is their temple. However, most of us live in crowded and crime-ridden cities where privacy necessary for a ritual is not easy to find. Besides, many rituals are performed under the Full Moon, so doing this outdoors may not be safe (unless you have a garden, but then, there are neighbors to consider). There is also the issue of weather. Therefore, an indoor altar is much more practical because you can concentrate on the ritual without having to worry about privacy, safety or rain. Indoor altars should be placed somewhere you are least likely to be disturbed, and where visitors are unlikely to see or hold your altar items.

2. Direction

Your altar can face any direction but the preferred direction is the East, where the Sun rises. However, during a ritual, whenever possible, try to face the quarter you need the most help from (e.g., North for finance, South for passion, etc.).

3. The style and size

As Wicca is a reconstructed religion of pre-Christian Europe, most of the Wiccan deities and rituals are based on those cultures. However, you may choose to follow beliefs of ancient or current Pagan religions from outside Europe, such as Hinduism, Taoism, African religions, etc., but try not to mix and match too many different items on your altar (or in your rituals).

So, if you feel drawn to Hindu deities and practices, stick to those—don't mix them with Celtic or African ones. In many ways, your altar is your ID and should reflect your spirituality and values, so the items you keep there speak for you.

Wicca For Beginners

The way you will decorate your altar will also depend on the effect you want to achieve, and resources you can set aside for this. There is no need to spend a lot of money on expensive Wicca tools and items because all you need for your altar you can easily find in your kitchen, your garden, or the local park. Wicca is about Nature, and Nature is all around us.

PART 3

Practical Wicca

Chapter 6
Becoming a Wiccan

How to Get Started?

A Wiccan is often described as a witch, but do you know what the word "witch" means? The literal translation of the word witch is "wise" because in ancient times witches were respected for their knowledge of healing herbs, as well as for their ability to perform magic that could heal or harm people. That's why witchcraft is also called "the craft of the wise."

However, when you become a Wiccan, you do not automatically become a witch. You can be part of the Wicca movement on many different levels, and there are many different traditions to choose from. But overall, a witch is someone interested in healing, someone who feels attracted to nature and feels close to Her, and someone who honors the Goddess.

Some traditions insist on initiation ceremonies for new members, while others don't. You can choose to belong to a coven or to be a solitary witch.

Eclectic Wicca is a non-traditional Wicca that doesn't fit into any specific category and followers of this tradition mix and match different traditions.

Coven Wicca is usually much more structured with sometimes very strict rules as to who and how one can join.

Solitary Wiccans are those who do not belong to a specific coven but do rituals and spells on their own. They may or may not follow a specific tradition.

Those who enjoy group work usually join a coven, but those who prefer working on their own or if there is no coven near where they live, decide to go solo. If you decide to be a solitary witch, you can still be in touch with other witches through various forums on the Internet and you can attend major festivals and ceremonies organized by local Wicca covens. As you'll be working on your own, you will have no one to consult for guidance so it's important you read as much about Wicca as you can, or subscribe to Wicca magazines and join Wicca forums.

Choose a path you feel most comfortable with or you can mix and match from different traditions. Start collecting items for your altar and learn how to cast a Circle and perform rituals. Choose one or two Sabbats to celebrate, and one Esbat you will celebrate every month (people usually choose the New or the Full Moon).

Start practicing visualization, for you will need this a lot. Start learning about herbs, crystals, the Elements. Identify the Goddess you'd like to work with and learn as much as you can about her. Develop your intuition and learn to trust it. And you're ready!

If you are new to Wicca, follow the guidelines for spells and rituals, but it is quite all right to come up with your own, as most witches eventually do.

Developing Skills and Knowledge

Although you can learn Wicca from books, magazines, blogs, forums, lectures, and other Wiccans, magic requires a certain level of psychic development which can be achieved through certain spiritual practices such as yoga breathing, repeating mantra, saying prayers, and other activities which raise your vibrations and make you more receptive to the world of Spirit.

Three simple steps to raise your vibrations:

1. **Develop your intuition**

You can do this by practicing visualization, by living in the present (rather than worrying about the future and feeling sad about the past), by learning to trust your gut feeling, and by learning to listen to your inner voice. If you have good intuition, you will easily pick up the vibes from your environment, and this can be very useful not just in spellwork, but in everyday life

2. **Meditate and visualize regularly**

People meditate in most unusual ways. Some do it by sitting for hours in a lotus position, others by gazing into a candle flame or an open fire, some prefer to focus on an object or picture of a deity, still others do it while making bread, walking, or gardening. Meditation is about switching off and becoming so relaxed that you become receptive to your subconscious, and how you do it is up to you.

3. Tune in with Nature

Nature is a great absorber of negativity, and being surrounded by trees, mountains, or big open spaces makes it easy to connect with your subconscious as well as with the world of Spirit. Take long, quiet walks in Nature as often as you can, listen to the sounds around you, and observe the season.

Although we all possess intuitive powers, most of us have ignored them for so long, they no longer exist. However, your intuition is not dead, it simply became dormant. The difficult part is persuading yourself to hear what your inner voice is telling you because it often isn't what you'd like to hear. However, the more you listen to your inner voice, the better at interpreting it you will become.

To successfully interpret the symbolism of colors, crystals, or herbs, start improving your knowledge of plant, crystal, and color symbolism. How to do it?

- **Learn about color therapy**

The symbolism of color is very important in ritual, so learn how you can use color to match your intent.

- **Learn about crystal therapy**

Crystals are an essential part of rituals, talismans, and altars. Find out as much as you can about their physical, healing, as well as magical properties.

- **Learn about herbs**

Traditionally, witches are healers, so start by learning about healing properties of a few common herbs, and gradually expand your knowledge to include all the herbs available locally. Start collecting or growing your own.

- **Learn about energy healing**

Your personal energy is your biggest asset. Protect yourself from those who steal it by making you feel drained, uncomfortable or "small." Avoid being around such people if you can; if you can't, spend as little time near them as possible.

Keeping a Book of Shadows

A Book of Shadows is a book where Wiccans keep notes about rituals, spells, magic potions, as well as personal experiences with some of these. This is a very personal book and should not be loaned or passed on to others. In fact, traditionally, a Witch's Book of Shadows is destroyed upon death.

Wicca covens usually have one such book which remains unchanged and is used to initiate new members.

A personal Book of Shadows that Wiccans are encouraged to keep is often called a journal because Wiccans use it to record their personal experiences with rituals, spells, and magic. To start keeping your Book of Shadows, start collecting information relevant to the Wicca way of life.

Seven things you could include in your Book of Shadows:

1. The Wheel of the Year.

2. The Sabbats and Esbats dates for each year.

3. The Elements and their symbols.

4. Ideas for spells and rituals you collected from books, the Internet, or learned about from other Wiccans. Make written notes of the spells you cast for yourself or others and what the results were, such as what changes happened and when. Make a note of how certain herbs, crystals, or colors affect you.

5. Make note of mantras, chants, or prayers you use or intend to use.

6. Make a note of items you still need to buy, or of ways to decorate your altar for different occasions.

7. Collect and keep interesting photos which help you get into a certain mood or which you can use as symbols in some of your spells (e.g., pictures or postcards of the full moon, sunrise, peaceful lake, a storm, certain animals, ancient trees, unusual rock formations, etc.).

Chapter 7

Spells

10 Spells to Get you Started

1. Worry banishing spell

You will need: 1 small black candle, 1 piece of paper

Cast your Circle or sit in front of the altar (where you have set up the tools for the ritual). Draw a pentacle on the paper and place it inside the Circle or on the altar. Invoke your deities. Light the candle and start chanting:

"(name your deities) I call on you to banish what is causing me harm. With this candle, please burn the harm away."

Visualize the cause of your anxiety, and as the candle burns and wax melts, imagine your worries disappearing. Wait for the candle to burn down, give thanks, and close the Circle.

2. Love spell to help you find your soulmate

You will need: 4 small red candles, 2 small white candles

Cast a Circle, or sit in front of your altar, facing North. Close your eyes, breathe slowly, relax. Focus on your desire. Open your eyes. Invoke the Goddess of love.

Slowly, invoke each of the elements—Earth, Fire, Air, and Water—placing a red candle at each of the quarters (North, South, East, West). Then, light two white candles and place them on each side of you, gaze at the flames, and say:

I pray to Goddess of love to bring into my life the soulmate that I crave and the love that I deserve.

Hold the white candles together until the two flames become one.

Say: As the flames come together, I bring my wish to pass.

Visualize your soulmate in as much detail as you can and stay with this image for a while. See yourself as you would like to feel once you find your true love—happy, confident, and loved. Then, blow out the white candles and say:

I release this intent into the Universe.

Wait for the red candles to burn down. Give thanks and close the Circle. Bury what was left of the white candles in the garden (or in a flower pot if you don't have a garden) and leave a small gift for the Goddess next to the spot where you buried the candles (e.g., birdseed, flowers, candies, a piece of crystal, etc.).

3. Headache relief spell

You will need: a glass of Full Moon water, 1 lavender-scented candle, 1 teaspoon lavender flowers, 1 piece clear quartz crystal.

Pour boiling water over the dry lavender flowers. Cast a Circle or sit in front of your altar. Light the candle, close your eyes, and relax. Inhale the lavender steam from the teacup and say:

"Flowers of purple, heal my head

I will not take to my bed

The pain will flee

O' rising stream take the pain with thee."

Sip the herbal infusion and feel yourself relaxing, and your headache going away. After you have drunk most of the tea, place the crystal in the remaining tea and say:

"Crystal Bright, Bring your shining Light

Take this pain to keep me sane

Right now I feel no mirth

Your power is from the Earth

Send this pain away and make my day!"

Remove the crystal from the cup and place it on your "third eye" (the area right between your eyebrows), lie down for ten minutes, and let the crystal absorb the pain. When you are ready (when the headache had gone and when the candle had burned down), give thanks and close the Circle. Wash the crystal under running water and put it away.

4. Warding off depression spell

You will need your favorite dry herbs or incense, 1 medium-sized yellow candle, some boiling water.

Perform this ritual only if you know that your altar will not be disturbed for three days. Charge the ritual tools you will use for this spell with your intent. Cast a Circle or sit in front of your altar. Focus on your intent, telling yourself how good it must be not to be depressed. Dispel any thoughts of fear, doubt, insecurity, or sadness.

Light the incense or pour boiling water over the herbs, and breathe in the aroma. Invoke the Goddess you want to work with. Imagine a bright yellow light coming down and enveloping you and your altar.

Light the candle, hold it in your hands, gaze at the flame, and direct your positive energy to it, saying:

As I light this candle, my life becomes bright and the darkness disappears. This candle brings hope and positive energy into my life, and as it burns, my spirits are lifting and I feel happier and more confident every minute. I am no longer depressed, lonely, and am free from depression.

For about ten minutes, visualize yourself being free from depression, then give thanks and close the Circle. Repeat this spell two more times over the next few days. On the last night, after you have closed the Circle, bury what has remained of the candle in the garden (or the flower pot if you don't have a garden). As you bury it, repeat: *I'm free of depression.*

5. Spell to banish anxiety

Crystals that work best for anxiety are citrine, amethyst, and hematite.

Keep your space (your home or your room, for example) clean and tidy. Regularly open the windows to let fresh air in. Place the crystals (citrine, amethyst, and hematite) in a prominent place in the room you use most. Put some salt in the corners of all your rooms, or in the room you spend the most time in. When you feel yourself sinking into a state of anxiety, get up, clap your hands, stamp your feet, or sing. Use lavender or chamomile incense sticks to clear the energy in your living space.

6. Ritual for the dead

When casting a Circle for the Samhain Sabbat, you can set the boundaries by marking them with flower petals and herbs such as rose, rosemary, juniper, bay, parsley, yew, and whatever other fresh flowers or herbs you can find on October 31st (this will largely depend on where you live).

Dim the lights. Cast a Circle and define the boundaries with herbs. Step inside. Mark the four quarters, invoke the Elements, and invoke the deities you want to work with for this spell. Light the candle. If you have a picture of the deceased, place it under the candle. If you have some of their possessions, place them next to the candle.

Focus on who you want to communicate with. Visualize this person, try to remember the sound of their voice, smell the perfume or aftershave they used, and feel them near you. Ask them to join you. Repeat these words while sprinkling the Circle (or the altar if you are using it instead of the Circle) with the flower petals, leaves, and springs:

The wheel of life turns,

The cycle of rebirth continues.

Those beyond life,

You are remembered today.

Repeat this several times, but if nothing happens, (i.e., if the deceased does not appear), don't push it.

Focus on what you want to achieve, such as who you are hoping to meet. Inhale the scent of fresh herbs, be as relaxed as you can.

If the deceased appears, ask them a question and wait for the answer. If you hear nothing, go to the next question. Do not ask more than three questions. When you are done, give thanks and close the Circle. Communing with the dead can be stressful and exhausting, so after the ritual, sit quietly for a few moments and have a glass of water to ground yourself.

7. Distance healing spell

You will need three white candles, a piece of clear quartz crystal, peppermint incense, a picture of the person you want to heal.

Decide which Goddess you are going to invoke for this healing spell. Cast a Circle or sit in front of your altar. Place the picture in the center of the Circle (or altar) and the crystal on top of it. Place the candles around it. Place the incense in front of you. Light the candles.

Invoke the Goddess and ask her to empower your spell. Look at the picture and focus on your intent. Raise your energy in the way that suits you most, (dancing, singing, drumming, or visualizing). When you feel you have raised enough energy, direct it toward the crystal. Visualize a protective ring of white light forming around that person, shielding them from disease, pain, and suffering.

When you are done, and when the candle had burned down, give thanks and close the Circle. Sit quietly for a few moments to ground yourself. Have a glass of water.

8. Money Spell

It's best to do this spell during a waxing Moon and on a Thursday (ruled by luck-bringing Jupiter).

You will need one small dark brown candle, a gold coin, or a dollar note (or whatever currency you'd like to receive money in).

Sit in a quiet room lit only by the moonlight. Carve the dollar sign into the candle (or whatever other currency you want to work with) and put it in a candle holder. Light the candle and while you gaze at the flame, visualize wealth and prosperity entering your life. Put the gold coin between your palms, rub it for a few moments, then hold it tight. Say the following three times:

May this fire bring me the money I desire.

Wait for the candle to burn down, thinking about what you would spend the money on. Keep the coin or dollar note you used in the ritual in your wallet or purse. If your luck hasn't changed in about six weeks, repeat the spell until it does.

9. **Job promotion spell**

This spell works best if performed during a waxing Moon and on a Sunday.

You will need one medium-sized gold candle.

Perform this ritual when you know you will not be disturbed for half an hour. Cast a Circle or sit in front of your altar. Charge the candle with your intent.

Light the candle and as you gaze at the flames, think about all the job achievements that you believe you should be rewarded for. Feel satisfied and proud of your achievements. Visualize yourself as you would like to be—appreciated, confident, promoted. See yourself in the new position and think about how the promotion would positively affect other aspects of your life. Repeat slowly three times:

This bright light will find a new position for me.

Wait until the candle has burned down naturally. Give thanks and close the Circle. If you are passed over for a promotion, repeat the spell using a bigger candle (so the ritual would last longer and you would spend more time aligning yourself to your intent).

10. **Disease Banishing Spell**

You will need a red or black cord, black candle, open fire, one big piece of clear quartz crystal.

Cast a Circle or sit in front of the altar. Place the crystal in the middle (of the Circle or the Altar) and the candle next to it. Light the candle. Bind the part of the body that requires healing (e.g., head, arm, leg, stomach) with the red or black cord. Focus on the affected part of the body. Say:

I bind the disease residing in (name the part of the body). May it leave my body forever. Great Goddess (name the deity you are invoking), please take the disease away. The disease is bound into the cord and flames will destroy it. So make it be!

Untie the cord and throw it immediately into the fire. Focus on your intent. Visualize the disease being destroyed with the flames. Focus on the burning cord until it had been devoured by the fire. Close your eyes and while you wait for the candle to burn down, visualize yourself free of pain forever. Give thanks and close the Circle.

Closure

We hope this book provided an introduction to the world of Wicca and that after reading it you feel uplifted and inspired.

Wicca religion is not based on strict doctrines and dogmas, but is more a way of life. Being a Wiccan is about aligning yourself with the living and non-living world and learning how to draw your power from Nature.

Wiccans believe that everything in the universe is connected by an intricate web of life and that even non-living objects, such as rivers, stars, the Moon, etc., have personal energy which can be tapped into.

Wiccans care for Earth and believe that balance, both within us and in our environment, is the key to health and wellbeing. Their deepest spiritual feelings focus on the natural world and this makes it easy for them to commune with Nature or identify with the plant or animal spirit guides.

Pagans find the sacred in the natural, rather than the man-created world, and worship their

Goddess in the open, with the sky being their temple and Mother Earth their chief deity.

Thanks to so-called progress, most of us have become alienated from the world we were once part of—which we today find threatening and continually try to conquer. On the other hand, Wicca encourages us to tune into our inner wisdom and harmonize our lives with the seasonal cycles, which can help us come to terms with the cycles of our own lives.

What perhaps best explains the reason for the rapidly growing numbers of Wicca followers across the world is that more and more people feel the need to slow down and pay attention to the world around them. Some people call it living mindfully; Wiccans call it being aligned with Nature.

Although Wicca is a reconstructed European religion of pre-Christian times, our knowledge about how ancients celebrated life and death comes as much from historical records as from the comparative studies of traditional cultures that continue to survive in the 21st century.

When you consider all the social changes our world has gone through and persecution that most of the Pagans suffered at one time or other, it's a miracle that pockets of paganism still survive in this day and age. Deep in the Amazonian jungles, across Siberia, and all over Africa, millions of Pagans nurture and protect their nature-based religion as the change of consciousness slowly spreads throughout the world, changing the mindset of people.

Practicing Wicca can be a very liberating experience because you realize it's possible to practice spirituality outside the limiting structures of an "organized" religion. On the other hand, as there are no set of rules and doctrines to fall back on, the learning and growing within this religion is entirely up to you.

Although this is only an introduction to Wicca beliefs and traditions, this is a lot of information for a beginner to take in, so revisit this book often until you become familiar with different concepts, traditions, and rituals.

Sometimes it's difficult to know if something is right for you or not. But, if after reading this book you can't wait to surrender to the rhythm of nature or align yourself with the phases of the moon, then something in this book triggered a Pagan inside you.

The beauty of Wicca is that it can be practiced in different ways and for different reasons, and as Scott Cunningham, who published one of the most successful books on Wicca pointed out, "Magic is not always serious or solemn. It is a joyous celebration and merging with the life-force."

Thank you

Before you go, I just wanted to say thank you for purchasing my book.

You could have picked from dozens of other books on the same topic but you took a chance and chose this one.

So, a HUGE thanks to you for getting this book and for reading all the way to the end.

Now I wanted to ask you for a small favor. **Could you please consider posting a review on the platform? Reviews are one of the easiest ways to support the work of authors.**

This feedback will help me continue to write the type of books that will help you get the results you want. So if you enjoyed it, please let me know.

Lastly, don't forget to grab a copy of your Free Bonus - my complete ***Law of Attraction: Attract What You Desire* Boxset**. If you want to learn how to harness the amazing magic of the Law of Attraction to manifest anything you want, this boxset is for you.

www.ingramcontent.com/pod-product-compliance
Lightning Source LLC
Chambersburg PA
CBHW071723020426
42333CB00017B/2368